LITTLE PIP EATS

THE COLOURS OF
THE RAINBOW

AMIE HARPER

MURDOCH BOOKS
SYDNEY · LONDON

To my husband, Phillip Harper, for cleaning up our messes
and putting up with our emotional ups and downs.

I'm lucky he's a patient man!

RED 6

YELLOW 12

PINK 18

GREEN 28

PURPLE 36

ORANGE 42

BLUE 50

WELCOME TO THE RAINBOW

Introducing food to babies is messy and fun, but the job is far from done once their infant days are behind them. The toddler years are where their curiosity and appetite really ramp up. As a qualified nutritionist, I know how important maintaining a balanced diet and lifestyle are to overall health and well-being. But as a mum, I also understand how overwhelming it can be to have someone's future relationship with food in your hands.

My first cookbook, *Baby Pip Eats*, was born out of my renewed interest in children's nutrition after having my first baby, Pip. My final year of university had been spent studying children's snacking behaviour at school, and then trying to implement healthy eating initiatives at local kindergartens. Around the same time I started introducing food to Pip, I noticed fellow mums and dads experiencing the 'what to cook' dilemma that faces every parent daily. I wanted to help eliminate this problem by sharing a few wholesome recipes that anyone could cook with some kitchen cupboard essentials and a few fresh ingredients.

Mealtimes at my house now include baby Jimmy, toddler Pip, my husband and me, so meals have to be easy and fun, as well as nutritious and tasty. This book is the next step on from *Baby Pip Eats*, with slightly more sophisticated recipes that bridge the transition from baby to toddler. The recipes here (unless otherwise indicated) are suitable for all ages, once chewing has developed. The focus is on encouraging a healthy diet through offering visually stimulating foods, which is why the recipes are divided by colour. Eating the rainbow when it comes to fruits and vegetables is one of the fundamental principles of good nutrition, it's also one of the easiest ways to incorporate a plethora of wholefood into the diet of your growing child, which is hugely important to their development. Offering a variety of colourful foods will pique your child's interest and encourage them to become more adventurous eaters. But that's not all: serving a variety of different textures will also stimulate them intellectually, through tactile learning, and physically, by encouraging mouth, jaw and tongue muscle development, which assists in speech development. All this from food!

I want this book to give parents confidence and a 'have a go' attitude when it comes to cooking for their kids. Preparing simple, wholesome foods and presenting them in a way that looks fun and exciting is easier than you might think.

Getting children involved with ingredient selection and meal preparation can really pay off. Pip loves helping me to select ingredients and prepare meals. She's my number 1 assistant! And I'm sharing a basic life skill that will serve her for the rest of her life. It's our responsibility as parents to give our kids the best possible start to life, and instil confidence, a love of cooking and a good understanding of food. Why not have fun doing it?

Raspberries, tomatoes, capsicums ... red foods are potent sources of vitamin C, folate and antioxidants thanks to nature's pigment, lycopene.

FLUFFY RASPBERRY PANCAKES

SOURCE OF: PROTEIN, DIETARY FIBRE, FOLATE & VITAMINS C & K
MAKES: APPROXIMATELY 24 SMALL PANCAKES
SERVES: 1 BABY/TODDLER & FAMILY OF 4

265 g (9¼ oz) self-raising flour
2 free-range eggs, separated, yolks lightly beaten
375 ml (13 fl oz/1½ cups) milk
300 g (10½ oz/1¼ cups) ricotta cheese
1 tablespoon butter or mild tasting olive oil
250 g (9 oz/2 cups) raspberries (or other berries)

Put the flour in a large bowl and make a well in the centre. Pour in the egg yolks, milk, 200 g (7 oz) of the ricotta and mix well. Whisk the egg whites in a clean bowl until soft peaks form. Fold the egg whites through the batter.

Heat the butter or oil in a large frying pan and spoon ¼-cup measures of the batter into the frying pan. Place 3 raspberries on each uncooked pancake and cook for 5 minutes, turning once, until lightly golden. Remove from the pan and repeat with remaining batter.

TIP: For a special and indulgent breakfast, add a spoonful of extra berries, lemon curd and mascarpone to each plate before serving.

RED CAPSICUM & CASHEW SAUCE

**SOURCE OF: PROTEIN, IRON, ZINC & MAGNESIUM (CASHEWS)
& VITAMIN C (RED CAPSICUM)
SERVES: 1 BABY/TODDLER & FAMILY OF 4**

3 red capsicums (peppers)
400 g (14 oz) unsalted cashews
25 g (1 oz/¼ cup) finely grated parmesan cheese

Preheat the oven to 180°C (350°F). Line a baking tray with baking paper. Place the capsicums on the lined baking tray and cook them for 25 minutes, or until slightly blackened and soft. Remove from the oven, place in a bowl and cover with plastic wrap. Set aside for 10 minutes.

Place the cashews on another baking tray and toast in the oven for 5 minutes, or until slightly golden. Remove from the oven and allow to cool completely.

Peel the capsicums and discard their skins, stems and seeds. Place the flesh in a food processor along with the cashews and parmesan. Pulse until smooth.

Serve with cooked pasta, or as a dip with steamed vegetables.

NOTE: This recipe contains nuts.

BAKED BEAN BREKKIE

SOURCE OF: DIETARY FIBRE, IRON & VITAMINS A & C
SERVES: 1 BABY/TODDLER & A FAMILY OF 4

olive oil
3 French shallots, finely chopped
2 garlic cloves, finely chopped
1 tablespoon finely chopped rosemary leaves
1 x 400 g (14 oz) tin butter beans, drained and rinsed
500 g (1 lb 2 oz) fresh tomatoes, roughly chopped
250 g (9 oz) cherry tomatoes
4 free-range eggs

Preheat the oven to 175°C (345°F). Heat the oil in a medium non-stick ovenproof pan or flameproof casserole dish over a medium heat. Add the shallot and cook for 3–5 minutes, or until softened and translucent, then add the garlic and cook for a further minute.

Add the rest of the ingredients, except the eggs, and bring everything to a gentle boil. Use a serving spoon to make four little wells in the bean mixture, then crack an egg into each well. Transfer the pan to the oven and cook for 15–20 minutes, or until the eggs are cooked to the desired doneness. Remove from the oven and allow to sit for 5 minutes before serving with fresh crusty bread.

CHECK: Cook eggs through completely for babies under 12 months and pregnant mothers.

Vibrant yellow foods help promote strong immune and digestive systems. They are high in alpha and beta carotenes, luetin and vitamin C. Sunshine on a plate.

CORN FRITTERS

SOURCE OF: PROTEIN, VITAMIN B-6, MAGNESIUM & CARBOHYDRATES
SERVES: 1 BABY/TODDLER & A FAMILY OF 4

3 corncobs, steamed for 5–8 minutes, or until tender
150 g (5½ oz/1 cup) self-raising flour
185 ml (6 fl oz/¾ cup) milk
2 free-range eggs
1 tablespoon olive oil

Once the corn is cool enough to handle, slice the kernels off each cob. Reserve some of the kernels for garnish, discard the cobs. Whisk the flour, milk and eggs together in a mixing bowl until smooth, then add the corn kernels.

Heat the olive oil in a large frying pan over a medium heat. Spoon ¼-cup measures of the batter into the pan and cook the fritters for 5 minutes, or until golden, turning them once. Move to a plate and keep warm in the oven while you make the rest of the fritters.

Serve warm, with the reserved corn kernels sprinkled on top. For a more substantial meal, serve with sliced avocado, bacon, fresh rocket (arugula) leaves and some feta cheese crumbled on top.

QUICK FRIED RICE & EASY OMELETTE

SOURCE OF: PROTEIN & ALL 9 ESSENTIAL AMINO ACIDS,
VITAMIN A, D & E & B12 (EGGS) & CARBOHYDRATES
SERVES: 1 BABY/TODDLER & A FAMILY OF 4

200 g (7 oz/1 cup) white rice
140 g (5 oz/1 cup) frozen peas
2 teaspoons olive oil or butter
1 brown onion, finely chopped
2 cloves garlic, crushed
4 middle-cut bacon rashers, finely chopped
1 carrot, peeled and finely chopped
8 free-range eggs (9 if you want to make a small omelette for your baby)

Cook the rice according to packet instructions, adding the peas
for the last 5 minutes of cooking. Drain and set aside.

Heat a large wok or non-stick frying pan over a medium heat. Add
1 tablespoon of olive oil and cook the onion and garlic until soft and fragrant.
Add the bacon and carrot, and cook for a further 5 minutes. Add the peas and
rice to the frying pan, stir gently then cook on a low heat for 3 minutes,
stirring occasionally. Remove from the heat.

Whisk 2 of the eggs with 1 tablespoon of water. Heat another tablespoon
of oil in a small non-stick frying pan over a medium heat. Pour the beaten
egg into the pan and stir, using a spatula, in a figure 8 motion. Cook for
1–2 minutes, until the egg is almost set before folding the omelette in half and
cooking for a further minute. Flip over once the egg is completely cooked.
Repeat 3 more times (or 4, if making a single-egg omelette just for baby)
with the remaining eggs and serve with fried rice.

**CHECK: Cook eggs through completely for babies
under 12 months and pregnant mothers.**

HAM & CHEESE FRITTATA

SOURCE OF: PROTEIN, VITAMINS A & C, POTASSIUM
MAKES: 6 SMALL OR 2 MEDIUM FRITTATAS, OR 1 LARGE FRITTATA
SERVES: 1 BABY/TODDLER & FAMILY OF 5

butter or oil, for greasing
10 free-range eggs
125 ml (7 fl oz/½ cup) milk
100 g (3½ oz/1 cup) coarsely grated cheddar cheese
100 g (3½ oz) ham, roughly chopped
60 g (2¼ oz/¼ cup) tomato relish

Preheat the oven to 175°C (345°F). Lightly grease six small ovenproof tins or dishes, approximately 12 x 8 x 4 cm (4½ x 3¼ x 1½ inches).

Whisk together the eggs and milk. Sprinkle the grated cheese and chopped ham into the prepared tins, reserving some cheese for sprinkling on top. Try to distribute them between the tins as evenly as possible. Divide the egg mixture between the tins evenly, making sure it covers the ham and cheese. Sprinkle over the remaining cheese and dollop a few teaspoons of relish around the top. Bake for 15–20 minutes, or until the egg is cooked through and lightly golden. Serve immediately, but allow to cool for babies and young children. If using cherry tomatoes, check that they have cooled sufficiently.

OPTIONAL FLAVOURS: Add some blanched broccoli florets, chopped cherry tomatoes and parsley to each tin before pouring in the egg mixture.

NOTE: For one large frittata, grease a baking tin or casserole dish approximately 25 x 28 x 7 cm (10 x 11¼ x 2¾ inches) and bake for 35 minutes.

Anthocyanin, a beneficial plant compound, gives strawberries and raspberries their vibrant colour. Pink foods are also rich in Vitamin C and antioxidants. But this chapter also embraces pink-hued fish and meat in all their protein-packed glory.

PINKY PORRIDGE

SOURCE OF: CARBOHYDRATES, VITAMIN C & DIETARY FIBRE
SERVES: 1 BABY/TODDLER & FAMILY OF 4

150 g (5½ oz/1½ cups) rolled oats
750 ml (26 fl oz/3 cups) milk of your choice, plus extra to serve
200 g (7 oz) raspberries or hulled strawberries
1 tablespoon chia seeds
flaked coconut, gently toasted

Put the oats and the milk in a non-stick saucepan over a medium heat and bring to a gentle boil, stirring occasionally. Once boiling, add most of the berries (save a few for serving) and stir gently. Place the lid on the saucepan, turn off the heat and leave to sit for 10 minutes.

Gently stir then serve, sprinkled with chia seeds, toasted coconut flakes, a few fresh berries and a little jug of extra milk for pouring over.

STRAWBERRY & CREAM SCONES

SOURCE OF: CARBOHYDRATES, VITAMIN C & DIETARY FIBRE
MAKES: ABOUT 9 SCONES

370 g (13 oz/2¼ cups) self-raising flour, plus extra for dusting
½ teaspoon baking powder
300 ml (10½ fl oz) thin (pouring) cream
1 ripe banana, mashed
1 egg, lightly beaten
200 g (7 oz) strawberries, hulled and quartered

Preheat the oven to 180°C (350°F). Line a baking tray with baking paper.

Combine the flour and baking powder in a large mixing bowl. Mix the wet ingredients together in another bowl then add the strawberries to this mixture. Make a well in the centre of the dry ingredients, pour in the wet mixture and use a butter knife to gently 'cut' the mixture together — not much, just enough to bring everything together. Do not over-mix.

Turn this mixture onto a lightly floured workbench and use clean hands to knead the dough gently, just enough to bring it together.

Pat the dough into a large round about 5 cm (2 inches) thick then transfer to the lined baking tray. Score the dough evenly into thirds horizontally and vertically (see opposite). Bake for 20 minutes, or until lightly golden. If you prefer, you can use a 5 cm (2 inch) cookie cutter to cut out the scones. Arrange them on the prepared tray and bake for 18–20 minutes.

Serve with Greek-style yoghurt or whipped cream and a spoonful of mashed berries (and a cup of tea, for you!).

TIP: For an earthier flavour, swap half the flour for spelt flour and add another ½ teaspoon of baking powder.

SLOW-COOKED PORK

SOURCE OF: PROTEIN, VITAMIN B-6, IRON, ZINC
SERVES: 1 BABY/TODDLER & FAMILY OF 4

2 tablespoons olive oil
8 French shallots, peeled
2 bay leaves
½ a bunch of sage
1.5 kg (3 lb 5 oz) pork brisket, blade or shoulder
100 ml (3½ fl oz) chicken stock (optional)
pinch of salt, optional

Preheat the oven to 120°C (235°F). Heat the olive oil over a medium heat in a flameproof casserole pot with a lid (make sure the pot is large enough to fit the piece of pork before you start). Add the shallots, herbs and pork to the pot. Cook for 5 minutes until the pork is lightly seared and golden then place the lid on the pot and put it in the oven. Cook for 3½–4 hours, checking every hour to make sure the pork hasn't dried out — you can add 100 ml (3½ fl oz) chicken stock or water if it looks a little too dry.

Once the time is up, transfer the pork to a carving board, cover with foil and leave to rest for 10 minutes. Using two forks, pull and shred the meat apart. Drizzle any cooking juices from the pot over the pork. Serve with mashed potato, peas and sauerkraut.

TIP: For a deeper flavour, roughly chop 3 carrots and 2 celery stalks and add them to the pot at the start of the cooking process with 125 ml (4 fl oz/½ cup) of chicken stock. The vegetables can be discarded at the end, or served with the meal if they are still holding together and not too fatty from soaking in the cooking juices.

PINK SALMON PASTA

SOURCE OF: OMEGA-3 FATTY ACIDS, PROTEIN & CARBOHYDRATES.
SERVES: 1 BABY/TODDLER & FAMILY OF 4

400 g (14 oz) dried pasta
2 tablespoons olive oil
1 bunch of broccolini, roughly chopped
1 brown onion, finely chopped
2 garlic cloves, finely chopped
2 salmon fillets, skin off and pinboned
juice and zest of 1 lemon
50 g (1¾ oz/½ cup) finely grated parmesan cheese, plus extra to serve
a few basil leaves, finely sliced

Cook the pasta in a large pot of boiling water until al dente. Remove from the heat and drain then stir through half the olive oil and set aside.

Place the broccolini in a large heatproof bowl and pour over enough boiling water to just cover. Allow to stand for 5 minutes then quickly refresh under cold water, drain well and set aside.

Heat a large frying pan over a medium heat with the remaining olive oil and add the onion and garlic. Cook until the onion is soft and fragrant then transfer it to a plate and return the pan to the heat.

Add the salmon fillets and cook, turning once, for 5 minutes, or until cooked through. Remove the pan from the heat and flake the salmon into smaller pieces — checking for any little bones as you go. Add the pasta, broccolini, onion and garlic mixture, lemon juice and zest, and parmesan to the pan with the salmon. Toss everything together quickly, then divide between your plates and serve immediately with a little finely chopped basil and extra grated parmesan sprinkled on top.

PIGGIES IN BLANKETS

SOURCE OF: PROTEIN, IRON, CARBOHYDRATES & VITAMIN B1
SERVES: 1 BABY/TODDLER & FAMILY OF 4

1 tablespoon olive oil
1 brown onion, finely chopped
3 garlic cloves, crushed
1 kg (2 lb 4 oz) minced (ground) pork
60 g (2¼ oz/1 cup lightly packed) fresh breadcrumbs
1 green apple, peeled and grated
2 carrots, finely grated
1 large zucchini (courgette), grated
2 free-range eggs, each one beaten and kept in separate bowls
6 sheets puff pastry
2 tablespoons sesame seeds, optional

Preheat the oven to 190°C (375°F). Line two oven trays with baking paper. Heat the olive oil in a large frying pan over a medium heat and cook the onion for 3–5 minutes, or until translucent. Add the garlic and cook for a further minute. Transfer to a medium bowl, allow to cool slightly, then add the mince, breadcrumbs, apple, carrot, zucchini and 1 egg. Mix together thoroughly using clean hands then divide into 12.

Place a pastry sheet onto a clean workbench and halve it lengthways. Place a ball of filling onto each pastry edge closest to you and form a log shape. Roll to enclose the filling in pastry, then brush each roll with some of the remaining beaten egg and sprinkle with sesame seeds. Slice each log into 6 pieces. Repeat with the rest of the pastry and mince. Place on the trays, 2 cm (¾ inches) apart and bake for 25 minutes, or until golden brown and cooked through.

Serve with tomato relish for a snack, or greens and peas for a more complete dinner. Freeze any extra rolls, uncooked, then bake from frozen as above.

Lettuces, broccoli, cabbage, celery, peas, zucchini and leafy greens are great sources of folic acid, magnesium and calcium. So much green goodness, so little time!

PIP'S FRAÎCHE GREEN DIP

SOURCE OF: MONO & POLYUNSATURATED FATS, VITAMINS A, D & K & CALCIUM
MAKES: ABOUT 2 CUPS

2 avocados, peeled and stone removed
250 g (9 oz/1 cup) crème fraîche or cottage cheese
zest and juice of ½ a lemon, optional
6 chives, snipped

Combine all of the ingredients except the chives in a blender, food processor or bowl and whiz or mash together with a fork until you have a smooth paste.

Serve this dip with roasted or steamed vegetables to suit your baby's age and chewing ability. This dip will keep for 2 days in the fridge if stored in an airtight container.

BROCCOLI & ZUCCHINI FRITTERS

SOURCE OF: PROTEIN, VITAMINS A, C & K, CALCIUM & POTASSIUM
MAKES: ABOUT 12 FRITTERS
SERVES: 1 BABY/TODDLER & FAMILY OF 4

½ a head of broccoli, finely chopped
40 g (1½ oz/¼ cup) frozen peas (or 200 g/7 oz fresh peas), optional
1 zucchini (courgette), coarsely grated
100 g (3½ oz) haloumi cheese, coarsely grated
25 g (1 oz/¼ cup) finely grated parmesan cheese
2 free-range eggs, lightly beaten
35 g (1¼ oz/¼ cup) self-raising flour
1 tablespoon mint, finely chopped
1 tablespoon olive oil or butter

Place the broccoli and peas (if using) in a bowl and cover with boiling water. Leave for 5 minutes then refresh under cold water, drain well and set aside.

Squeeze any excess liquid from the zucchini using a tea towel or absorbent paper towel. Combine the vegetables with all of the remaining ingredients, except the oil, in a large bowl and mix well.

Heat the oil in a large non-stick frying pan over a medium heat. Add ¼-cup measures of the mixture to the pan and press down gently. Cook for 5 minutes, turning once, until golden on both sides. Transfer to a plate and keep warm while you cook the rest of the fritters. Serve immediately with a spoonful of plain yogurt, or refrigerate in an airtight container and enjoy as a healthy snack. These will keep for 2 days.

TIP: Serve with 2 boiled or poached eggs per adult for a filling meal with extra protein, and 1 egg for each little one. Make sure eggs are cooked through completely for babies under 12 months and pregnant mothers.

MUSHY PEA RISOTTO

SOURCE OF: DIETARY FIBRE, PROTEIN, VITAMINS A & K & FOLATE
SERVES: 1 BABY/TODDLER & FAMILY OF 4

220 g (7¾ oz/1 cup) medium grain brown rice, rinsed and drained (see note)
280 g (10 oz/2 cups) fresh or frozen peas
1 tablespoon olive oil
1 brown onion, finely chopped
2 garlic cloves, chopped
1.13 litres (39 fl oz/4½ cups) chicken stock (homemade or reduced salt)
45 g (1¾ oz/½ cup) parmesan cheese, coarsely grated
80 g (2¾ oz) goat's cheese, optional
1 small handful of flat-leaf (Italian) parsley or mint, finely chopped
freshly ground black pepper

Add the rice to a medium saucepan of boiling water then reduce the heat and simmer for 15 minutes. Drain and set aside.

Cook the peas in boiling water for 5 minutes. Purée half of the peas (or all of the peas if cooking for babies who haven't yet developed their chewing capability). Set aside.

Heat the oil in a large saucepan over a medium heat and add the onion. Cook until translucent, then add the garlic and half of the cooked rice. Cook, stirring, for a further minute. Add 1 cup of stock at a time, stirring occasionally, and adding more when almost all of the liquid has evaporated. This will take about 25–30 minutes. Once the rice is cooked through, remove the saucepan from the heat and stir through the pea purée and peas, parmesan, goat's cheese, chopped herbs and a little pepper.

NOTE: You can also use short-grain brown or white rice. If using white rice, reduce the amount of liquid by 185 ml (6 fl oz/¾ cup) and then skip the par-cooking step.

GREEN SEED MUESLI SLICE

EAT ME FROM: 12 MONTHS AND UP (SEE NOTE)
SOURCE OF: B VITAMINS, MAGNESIUM & POTASSIUM, FOLATE
MAKES: 1 SLICE TRAY

65 g (2½ oz/1 cup) shredded coconut
145 g (5½ oz/1 cup) sunflower kernels
155 g (5¾ oz/1 cup) pepitas
25 g (1 oz/1 cup) puffed rice
80 g (2¾ oz/½ cup) dried fruit (I used chopped dates)
40 g (1½ oz/¼ cup) black chia seeds
1 tablespoon flaxseeds
1 teaspoon vanilla extract
2 teaspoons ground cinnamon
80 g (2¾ oz) butter
120 g (4¼ oz) honey

Preheat the oven to 180°C (350°F). Line a baking tray with baking paper. Combine all of the ingredients except the butter and honey in a large bowl.

Melt the butter in a saucepan and add the honey. Stir gently then remove from the heat. Pour this melted mixture evenly over the mixture in the bowl. Stir until combined then spread the mixture evenly onto the prepared baking tray so it's an even thickness of about 2 cm (¾ inch).

Bake for 20 minutes, or until lightly golden. Remove from the tray and allow to cool completely before slicing. These keep for up to a week in an airtight container. And, if you like, you can also double-wrap individual slices in plastic wrap, pop them into an airtight container and freeze them for up to 3 months.

NOTE: Not recommended for babies under 12 months because of the honey included in this recipe. See note on page 52 for more information.

Purple means power! Foods like eggplant, beetroot and plums are full of antioxidants, rich in Vitamin C and full of dietary fibre. Stock up on purple foods whenever you can.

BABA GHANOUSH

SOURCE OF: DIETARY FIBRE, PROTEIN, CALCIUM
MAKES: 1 LARGE JAR
SERVES: 1 BABY/TODDLER & FAMILY OF 4 AS A SNACK

2 large eggplants (aubergines)
130 g (4¾ oz/½ cup) plain yoghurt
juice and zest of a lemon
1 tablespoon hulled tahini (sesame seed paste)
1 garlic clove
salt and pepper, to taste
2 tablespoons finely chopped flat-leaf (Italian) parsley
2 tablespoons finely chopped mint
1 tablespoon extra virgin olive oil, to serve

Preheat the oven to 200°C (400°F). Line a large tray with baking paper. Place the eggplants onto the lined tray and roast in the oven for 30 minutes, or until soft. Remove from the oven and allow to cool slightly. Halve each eggplant, scoop the flesh into a food processor and discard the skin. Blitz the eggplant with all the other ingredients except the herbs and the oil until smooth.

Top with the herbs, olive oil and serve with some fresh bread on the side. I also like to top this with pepitas and lemon zest for added crunch and flavour, and serve with grilled haloumi (cut into shapes, if you like).

GREEN SEED MUESLI SLICE

EAT ME FROM: 12 MONTHS AND UP (SEE NOTE)
SOURCE OF: B VITAMINS, MAGNESIUM & POTASSIUM, FOLATE
MAKES: 1 SLICE TRAY

65 g (2½ oz/1 cup) shredded coconut
145 g (5½ oz/1 cup) sunflower kernels
155 g (5¾ oz/1 cup) pepitas
25 g (1 oz/1 cup) puffed rice
80 g (2¾ oz/½ cup) dried fruit (I used chopped dates)
40 g (1½ oz/¼ cup) black chia seeds
1 tablespoon flaxseeds
1 teaspoon vanilla extract
2 teaspoons ground cinnamon
80 g (2¾ oz) butter
120 g (4¼ oz) honey

Preheat the oven to 180°C (350°F). Line a baking tray with baking paper. Combine all of the ingredients except the butter and honey in a large bowl.

Melt the butter in a saucepan and add the honey. Stir gently then remove from the heat. Pour this melted mixture evenly over the mixture in the bowl. Stir until combined then spread the mixture evenly onto the prepared baking tray so it's an even thickness of about 2 cm (¾ inch).

Bake for 20 minutes, or until lightly golden. Remove from the tray and allow to cool completely before slicing. These keep for up to a week in an airtight container. And, if you like, you can also double-wrap individual slices in plastic wrap, pop them into an airtight container and freeze them for up to 3 months.

NOTE: Not recommended for babies under 12 months because of the honey included in this recipe. See note on page 52 for more information.

MINI MOUSSAKAS

SOURCE OF: IRON, PROTEIN, DIETARY FIBRE & VITAMINS B2 & B12
MAKES: 6-8 MINI MOUSSAKAS
SERVES: 1 BABY/TODDLER & FAMILY OF 4

olive oil, for frying
1 onion, finely chopped
3 garlic cloves, finely chopped
1 tablespoon oregano, chopped
500 g (1 lb 2 oz) lean minced (ground) lamb
1 x 600 g (1 lb 5 oz) jar tomato passata
3 large or 4 small eggplants, sliced horizontally 1 cm (¾ inch) thick
260 g (9¼ oz/1 cup) plain yoghurt
1 egg yolk
200 g (7 oz) cheddar cheese, coarsely grated

Preheat the oven to 180°C (350°F). Heat 1 tablespoon of olive oil in a large frying pan over a medium heat and cook the onion, garlic and oregano until soft and fragrant. Add the mince and cook until lightly browned. Add the passata and simmer for 15 minutes.

Heat another large frying pan over a medium heat. Add 2 tablespoons of olive oil and fry the eggplant slices, in batches, for 3 minutes each side, or until lightly golden. Remove from the pan and place on paper towel. Whisk the yoghurt with the egg yolk until combined.

Line the bases and sides of six 10 cm (4 inch) individual ramekins with the slices of eggplant. Spoon the meat sauce into each ramekin until three-quarters full then pour the yoghurt sauce on top of the meat. Sprinkle grated cheese over each one, and then bake for 20–25 minutes, or until lightly golden.

BEETROOT SALAD BAKED POTATOES

SOURCE OF: PROTEIN, CARBOHYDRATES, DIETARY FIBRE, POTASSIUM & VITAMINS A, C & K
SERVES: 1 BABY/TODDLER & FAMILY OF 4

8 baking potatoes
1 head of broccoli, stalk trimmed and finely chopped, head broken into small florets
140 g (5 oz/1 cup) frozen or fresh peas
2 carrots, washed and coarsely grated
3 beetroots (beets), scrubbed and coarsely grated
1 x 400 g (14 oz) tin chickpeas, drained and rinsed
100 g (3½ oz) cheddar cheese, coarsely grated
100 g (3½ oz) plain yoghurt (optional)

Preheat the oven to 180°C (350°F). Wrap each potato in foil and place on a baking tray. Roast for 50–55 minutes, or until a knife goes through easily.

Blanch the broccoli and peas in boiling water for 2–3 minutes then refresh under cold water and drain well.

Unwrap the potatoes then divide them between the serving plates. Top with the cooked broccoli and peas as well as the carrot, beetroot, chickpeas, cheese and a dollop of yoghurt, if using, before serving.

Carotenoid is a fat-soluble ingredient found in kid-friendly favourites like carrots, pumpkin, sweet potato and oranges. Great for eyes, skin and for building immunity.

MINI CARROT, CHEDDAR & THYME ROSTIS

SOURCE OF: VITAMIN A & DIETARY FIBRE
MAKES: 14–16 MINI FRITTERS
SERVES: 1 BABY/TODDLER & FAMILY OF 4

3 carrots, peeled and coarsely grated
80 g (2¾ oz) cheddar cheese, grated
1 teaspoon thyme leaves, finely chopped
1 egg, lightly beaten
40 g (1½ oz/¼ cup) spelt flour or 35 g (1¼ oz/¼ cup) plain (all-purpose) flour
1 tablespoon butter or olive oil

Combine the carrot, cheddar, thyme, egg and flour in a mixing bowl. Heat a non-stick frying pan over medium heat and add the butter or olive oil. Add teaspoons of the rosti batter to the pan and press down gently with the back of the spoon to flatten slightly. Cook, turning once, for 5 minutes, or until golden. Serve with baby basil leaves, if you like.

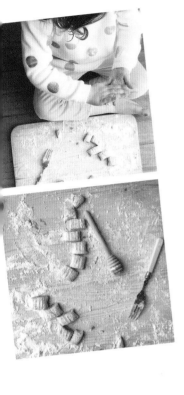

SWEET POTATO GNOCCHI

SOURCE OF: VITAMIN A & C, DIETARY FIBRE
SERVES: 1 BABY/TODDLER AND FAMILY OF 4

400 g (14 oz) sweet potato (2 small or 1 large)
185 g (6½ oz/1¼ cups) plain (all-purpose) flour, you may need
  a tablespoon or two more if the mixture is too wet
1 egg yolk
25 g (1 oz/¼ cup) parmesan cheese, finely grated (optional)

Preheat the oven to 190°C (375°F). Line a baking tray with baking paper. Roast the sweet potatoes (whole) for 50 minutes, or until soft when pierced with a skewer. Remove from the oven and, once cool, remove their skins.

Combine the cooled sweet potato flesh with the flour, egg yolk and parmesan, if using, in a mixing bowl. Place the dough on a lightly floured workbench and knead lightly. Divide evenly into four balls. Roll each ball gently into a 2 cm (¾ inch) thick sausage log. Slice the logs evenly into 2 cm pieces, press down gently on each with a fork, then set aside.

Cook the gnocchi in a large pan of boiling water until all of them rise to the surface. Drain. Serve with your favourite sauce such as a creamy mushroom sauce (see below) or basil pesto.

FOR THE PERFECT SAUCE WITH THIS GNOCCHI: Heat a tablespoon of olive oil in a frying pan over a medium heat. Add a chopped onion and cook for 5 minutes, or until translucent. Add 2 crushed garlic cloves and cook for a further minute before adding 200 g (7 oz) of sliced button mushrooms and a small handful of thyme. Cook for 5 minutes, or until softened. Add 300 ml (10½ fl oz) of thin (pouring) cream and bring to a gentle simmer. Reduce the heat and cook for 5 minutes. Stir through a small handful of finely grated parmesan and serve with the gnocchi.

BAKED FREGOLA WITH PUMPKIN

SOURCE OF: VITAMIN A, DIETARY FIBRE & CARBOHYDRATES
SERVES: 1 BABY/TODDLER & FAMILY OF 4

1 tablespoon olive oil
1 brown onion, finely chopped
2 garlic cloves, crushed
240 g (8½ oz/1½ cups) fregola (round pasta, similar to Israeli cous cous)
½ a kent pumpkin, peeled and roughly chopped
1 litre (35 fl oz/4 cups) water or chicken stock (homemade or reduced salt)
80 g (2¾ oz) goat's feta cheese
small handful of basil leaves
freshly ground black pepper, to taste

Preheat the oven to 180°C (350°F). Heat a large, deep non-stick frying pan over a medium heat. Add the olive oil and onion and cook for 2 minutes, or until the onion is soft. Add the garlic and cook for a further minute, or until fragrant.

Add the fregola, pumpkin, water or stock to the pan and bring to the boil. Cover with the lid then transfer to the oven and cook for 25–30 minutes, or until the fregola is al dente.

Sprinkle with the feta and the basil, then season with pepper to taste before serving.

CARROT CAKE

SOURCE OF: VITAMIN A & C, DIETARY FIBRE & CALCIUM
MAKES: 1 CAKE, APPROXIMATELY 16 SLICES

250 ml (9 fl oz/1 cup) mild tasting olive oil
150 g (5½ oz/¾ cup, lightly packed) muscovado (dark brown) sugar
3 free-range eggs
3 carrots, coarsely grated
½ teaspoon bicarbonate of soda (baking soda)
260 g (9¼ oz/1¾ cups) self-raising flour

Orange cream cheese icing
500 g (1 lb 2 oz) cream cheese, at room temperature
juice and zest of 2 oranges, at room temperature
40 g (1½ oz/¼ cup) pepitas

Preheat the oven to 175°C (345°F). Line the base and side of
a round 18 cm (7 inch) cake tin with baking paper.

Whisk the oil and sugar together in a large mixing bowl until completely
combined. Whisk in the eggs, one at a time, until combined. Mix the bicarb
and flour together, then sift into the mixture and stir until combined. Pour
the batter into the prepared cake tin and bake for 50 minutes, or until
a skewer inserted into the centre of the cake comes out clean.

Remove from the oven and allow to stand for 10 minutes before turning
out onto a wire rack to cool completely before icing.

Beat the cream cheese for 1–2 minutes with an electric mixer. Add half of the
orange juice and zest and beat for a further minute. Add a tablespoon extra
of juice if needed, to get the desired consistency.

Slice the cake in half horizontally. Spoon and spread icing all over the bottom
half. Place the other half of the cake on top and then spread the remaining
icing on the top of the cake and around the side, if you like. Sprinkle over the
remaining orange zest and the pepitas before serving.

The hues of blueberries, blue carrots and potatoes indicate the presence of powerful antioxidants that protect against cell damage.

BLUEBERRY ICE CREAM

SOURCE OF: CALCIUM, DIETARY FIBRE, MANGANESE & VITAMINS C & K
SERVES: 1 BABY/TODDLER & FAMILY OF 4

300 g (10½ oz) blueberries
390 g (13¾ oz/1½ cups) plain yoghurt
250 ml (9 fl oz/1 cup) milk
90 g (3¼ oz/¼ cup) honey (optional, see note below)
150 g (5½ oz) raspberries and/or blueberries, for serving

Add most of the blueberries, the yoghurt, milk and honey to a blender and blitz until smooth. Pour the mixture into an ice-cream machine and follow the manufacturer's instructions. Alternatively, pour the mixture into a freezer-safe container, seal and freeze for 2–4 hours. Blitz again in the blender to soften before serving with extra berries.

CHECK: For babies under 12 months, omit the honey and add 8 to 10 pitted dates to the blender for natural sweetness. See note on page 52 for more information about honey.

TIP: Ice-cream machines and frozen bowl attachments for stand mixers will yield a superior texture due to the mixing and chilling that occurs.

BLUEBERRY, DATE AND BANANA SMOOTHIE

SOURCE OF: PROTEIN, DIETARY FIBRE, OMEGA -3 FATTY ACIDS & VITAMIN C
SERVES: 1 BABY/TODDLER & FAMILY OF 4

250 g (9 oz) blueberries
1 tablespoon chia seeds
3 ripe bananas
6 dates, pitted and chopped
750 ml (26 fl oz/3 cups) milk
260 g (9¼ oz/1 cup) plain yoghurt
135 g (4¾ oz/1 cup) ice cubes
ground cinnamon, to serve
honey, to serve (optional, see note)

Reserve 2 tablespoons of the blueberries and 1 teaspoon of the chia seeds for serving. Place the rest of the ingredients in a large blender and blitz until smooth.

Divide between your glasses and serve sprinkled with the extra blueberries, chia seeds and a few pinches of cinnamon.

NOTE: Honey can contain spores of a bacterium called *Clostridium botulinum*, which can germinate in a baby's immature digestive system and cause infant botulism, a rare but potentially fatal illness. Honey should not be given to babies under 12 months old. In adults and children over 12 months, the microorganisms normally found in the intestine keep this bacteria from growing.

PLUM & LAMB TAGINE

SOURCE OF: IRON, PROTEIN, & DIETARY FIBRE
SERVES: 1 BABY/TODDLER & FAMILY OF 4 WITH LEFTOVERS

1 tablespoon olive oil
about 1 kg (2 lb 4 oz) lamb shoulder meat, roughly chopped and fat trimmed
1 brown onion, roughly chopped
3 garlic cloves, finely chopped
1 cm (½ inch) ginger, peeled and finely chopped
1 tablespoon ground cumin
1 tablespoon ground coriander
2 teaspoons ground turmeric
1 cinnamon quill
1 large handful of coriander
1 large handful of mint
500 ml (17 fl oz/2 cups) salt-reduced chicken stock or water
2 x 400 g (14 oz) tin chickpeas, rinsed and drained
1 x 400 g (14 oz) tin chopped tomatoes
10 plums, halved and de-stoned (or 10 fresh or dried apricots or pitted dates)
35 g (1¼ oz/¼ cup) slivered almonds, toasted and chopped
zest and juice of 1 lemon

Heat the oil in a large casserole pan over a medium heat then brown the lamb in batches. Remove and set aside. Fry the onion in the pan for 2–3 minutes, then add the garlic, ginger and spices. Cook for a further minute until soft and fragrant. Return the meat to the pan and add half of the herbs, the stock, chickpeas, tomatoes and plums. Stir gently, cover, and cook over a low heat for 4 hours, or until the meat is soft and pulls apart easily.

Serve on a bed of sweet potato mash with chopped almonds, lemon zest and a squeeze of lemon juice. Scatter over coriander and mint leaves to finish.

NOTE: This recipe contains nuts.

Published in 2017 by Murdoch Books, an imprint of Allen & Unwin

Murdoch Books Australia
83 Alexander Street,
Crows Nest NSW 2065
Phone: +61 (0)2 8425 0100
murdochbooks.com.au
info@murdochbooks.com.au

Murdoch Books UK
Ormond House,
26–27 Boswell Street,
London, WC1N 3JZ
Phone: +44 (0) 20 8785 5995
murdochbooks.co.uk
info@murdochbooks.co.uk

For Corporate Orders & Custom Publishing contact
Noel Hammond, National Business Development Manager,
Murdoch Books Australia

Publisher: Jane Morrow
Editorial Manager: Katie Bosher
Design Manager: Madeleine Kane
Design concept: Alice Gleadow
Production Manager: Rachel Walsh

Text © Amie Harper 2017
The moral rights of the author have been asserted.
Design © Murdoch Books 2017
Photography © Amie Harper 2017

A cataloguing-in-publication entry is available from the catalogue
of the National Library of Australia at nla.gov.au.

ISBN 978 1 74336 853 4 Australia
ISBN 978 1 74336 854 1 UK

A catalogue record for this book is available from the British Library.

Colour reproduction by Splitting Image Colour Studio Pty Ltd,
Clayton, Victoria
Printed by Hang Tai Printing Company, China

IMPORTANT: Those who might be at risk from the effects of
salmonella poisoning (the elderly, pregnant women, young children
and those suffering from immune deficiency diseases) should
consult their doctor with any concerns about eating raw eggs.

OVEN GUIDE: You may find cooking times vary depending on the
oven you are using. For fan-forced ovens, as a general rule, set the
oven temperature to 20°C (70°F) lower than indicated in the recipe.

MEASURES GUIDE: We have used 20 ml (4 teaspoon) tablespoon
measures. If you are using a 15 ml (3 teaspoon) tablespoon, add an
extra teaspoon of the ingredient for each tablespoon specified.

**All recipes are based on the author's food journey of introducing
her baby and toddler to solid foods from the age of 6 months.
All props are author's own and are for visual purposes only.
Never leave your baby alone while feeding, and make sure all
foods are finely chopped, puréed and steamed to coincide
with your baby's age and chewing ability to prevent choking.**

USEFUL REFERENCES

AUSTRALIA
World Health Organization
who.int/nutrition/topics/infantfeeding_recommendation/en
Australian Breastfeeding Association breastfeeding.asn.au
Dietitians Association of Australia daa.asn.au
**The Royal Australasian College of Physicians
(Paediatrics and Child Health Division)** racp.edu.au
The Royal Children's Hospital, Melbourne rch.org.au
The Royal Australian College of Immunology
Food & allergy information
Australasian Society of Clinical Immunology and Allergy
allergy.org.au

UK
Unicef unicef.org.uk
National Health Service nhs.uk
The Association of UK Dietitians
bda.uk.com

USA
**American Academy
of Pediatrics** aap.org
Breastfeeding USA
breastfeedingusa.org
Healthy Children
healthychildren.org